DEADLY DIS

Terrorist Attacks

Disaster & Survival

Mara Miller

Enslow Publishers, Inc.

40 Industrial Road	PO Box 38
Box 398	Aldershot
Berkeley Heights, NJ 07922	Hants GU12 6BP
USA	UK

http://www.enslow.com

To the victims of terrorism and their families
May they and the world find peace.
—MM

Library of Congress Cataloging-in-Publication Data:

Miller, Mara, 1968–
    Terrorist attacks : disaster & survival / Mara Miller.— 1st ed.
        p. cm. — (Deadly disasters)
    Includes bibliographical references and index.
    ISBN 0-7660-2385-0
    1. Terrorism—Juvenile literature. 2. Terrorists—Juvenile literature. I. Title.
II. Series.
    HV6431.M573 2005
    303.6'25—dc22
                                            2004011701

To Our Readers: We have done our best to make sure all Internet Addresses in this book were active and appropriate when we went to press. However, the author and the publisher have no control over and assume no liability for the material available on those Internet sites or on other Web sites they may link to. Any comments or suggestions can be sent by e-mail to comments@enslow.com or to the address on the back cover.

Illustration Credits: Associated Press, Al Jazeera, p. 28; Associated Press, AP, pp. 1, 9, 15, 22, 23, 25, 26, 29, 32, 33, 34 (inset), 36, 37; Associated Press, The Daily Progress, p. 8; Associated Press, John Labriola, p. 11; Associated Press, KHBS KHOG, p. 4; Associated Press, NTV, p. 17; Associated Press, Office of Homeland Security, p. 38; Associated Press, Pool Photo, p. 31; Associated Press, USMC, p. 21; Associated Press, The Washington Post, p. 34; Enslow Publishers, Inc., p. 7.

Cover Illustration: Associated Press, AP

Contents

The North Tower of the World Trade Center burns as a plane is about to hit the South Tower. Investigators later noted that the terrorists intentionally tilted the plane to cause as much damage as possible to the building.

Terrorism Strikes

AT 8:46 A.M. ON SEPTEMBER 11, 2001, A BOEING 767 airplane slammed into the World Trade Center's North Tower in New York City. It signaled the start of one of the deadliest acts of terrorism ever. A fiery hole gaped open. Smoke billowed against a nearly picture-perfect sky.

Photojournalist David Handschuh heard the call for firefighters and followed the Rescue One fire truck to the scene. "It was eerie and quiet on the street . . . You could hear the flames crackling and the glass breaking. You could see the debris falling," Handschuh remembered.[1]

He thought the plane crash was an accident. Many survivors, reporters, and TV viewers across the United States reacted the same way.

At 9:03, a second plane crashed into the South Tower.

"I saw a plane flying low," said Jim Gialamas. "[The plane] was wobbly . . . The wings were slanted and we saw it hit from the south. We saw the plane disappear, and then smoke and flames."[2]

This time it was clear. The United States was under attack by terrorists.

As people rushed out of the World Trade Center buildings, firefighters and police rushed in. They guided people through the smoky corridors and stairwells.

Judy Wein escaped from the seventy-eighth floor of the South Tower. "We saw the firefighters coming up," she recalled. "[T]hey would ask us, what floor did you come from? We told them, 78, and there's lots of people badly hurt up there."[3]

Jim Gertenberg was trapped on the eighty-sixth floor of the North Tower. "I don't know if I'm going to get out of it," he told a friend on the phone. "You have to take care of everyone for me."[4]

At 9:21 A.M., the Federal Aviation Administration halted flights throughout the United States. It was the first time in history that all air traffic was stopped. But there were still planes in the air and two of them were hijacked.

On board American Airlines Flight 77, Barbara Olson called her husband. She said that men with knives and box cutters had hijacked the plane and herded the passengers to the back.[5]

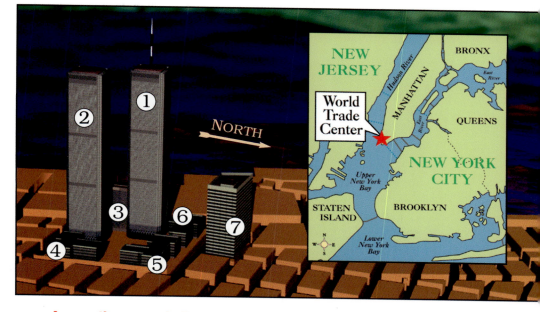

Among the seven buildings that made up the World Trade Center were the North Tower (1 World Trade Center), the South Tower (2 World Trade Center), and the Marriott Hotel (3 World Trade Center). The day of the attacks, 7 World Trade Center collapsed a few hours after the North and South Towers.

Less than ten minutes later, her plane made a near full circle turn and descended 2,200 feet. It plunged into the Pentagon, the United States center for defense, at about 530 miles per hour.[6]

Navy Captain Charles Fowler heard a deafening roar. "You could feel the building shake," he later said. "You knew it was a major explosion . . . Tons of smoke was coming up from the wedge—lots of black and gray smoke."[7]

Members of the Fairfax County, Virginia Search and Rescue Team approach the Pentagon to look for survivors.

People evacuated government buildings. The nation's capital was under attack. What would be hit next?

Back in New York, the South Tower collapsed. Boris Ozersky had fled down seventy flights of stairs and was just outside when the tower fell. "I just got blown somewhere, and then it was total darkness."[8]

A plume of smoke, ash, and debris exploded down the street. "I started to run," said reporter Susan Harrigan. "Everything turned black outside. All the lights went off. The air was thick with debris and ash."[9]

Jim Gertenberg, still trapped in the North Tower, got a hold of his wife. "I love you," he told her. "I love Nicole," he said about his two-year-old daughter.[10] Shortly thereafter the line went dead.

The North Tower had collapsed. It was 10:28—an hour and forty-two minutes after the first plane struck and thousands of lives were lost.

They Were Heroes

United Airlines Flight 93 was in the air about an hour when a voice said over the intercom, "We have a bomb

on board."[11] Those in the cabin soon realized that terrorists were in control of the plane.

Passengers called loved ones from the plane. According to the *9/11 Commission Report*, they reported that "a passenger had been stabbed and two people were lying on

Tons of steel and other debris come crashing down as the South Tower of the World Trade Center collapses.

the floor of the cabin, injured or dead."[12] They were told about the fatal flights in New York City.

"If we are going to crash into something . . . let's not let that happen," Jeremy Glick told his wife. "Our best chance is to fight these people, rather than accept it."[13]

Glick and a group of passengers decided to stop the hijackers from reaching a fourth target. At 9:57, the passenger assault began. The cockpit recorder captured sounds of the revolt—loud thumps, crashes, shouts, and the breaking of glasses and plates. At 10:02 a hijacker yelled, "Pull it down, Pull it down!"[14]

Shortly thereafter, the jet crashed in a field in Shanksville, Pennsylvania. All forty-four passengers died. While no bomb was found in the wreckage, the plane was only twenty minutes from Washington, D.C., the nation's capital. The passengers had stopped the plane from being used to attack another target.

There were other heroes that day. Strangers helped each other exit the Twin Towers. Fellow employees carried a woman who needed crutches down sixty-eight flights of stairs.

Firefighters sped to the scene. The team David Handschuh followed waved to him as they put on their gear. None of those eleven firefighters got back out alive. Over three hundred firefighters perished as the Twin Towers collapsed. They died trying to save others.

As workers came down the stairs of the Twin Towers, firefighters were charging up to rescue any remaining people. Engine 18 firefighter Mike Kehoe, pictured here, was able to escape the building before it collapsed.

In the months that followed, people combed through the wreckage. Others donated money, food, blood, supplies, and countless hours of hard work.

How Has Terrorism Changed Us?

According to the *9/11 Commission Report*, 3,212 people died in the attacks on September 11, 2001, or 9/11/2001. The victims came from over ninety countries.[15] The attacked buildings were symbols of freedom, trade, prosperity, and security. People came together after 9/11, but many of them were changed.

11

"When the power grid went out on the East Coast, my first thought was terrorism," said Long Island resident Mary Jo Fox. "I would not have thought that before 9/11."[16] However, the massive power outage on August 14, 2003, was not caused by terrorism.

Combating terrorism became a national emergency. President Bush created the Department of Homeland Security and declared a war on terrorism. This was a new kind of war. A war not against a nation, but against small groups of people called cells that could operate independently and move almost without detection.

People wanted to know who had carried out the attack on 9/11. Suspicions landed on Osama bin Laden and his terrorist group Al Qaeda. As the evidence grew, President Bush stated that he wanted Osama bin Laden brought to justice and recalled the Old West's "Wanted: Dead or Alive" signs.[17]

Bin Laden responded with joy at the destruction of the Twin Towers. In a taped statement he said, "[America's] greatest buildings were destroyed, thank God for that. There is America, full of fear from its north to its south, from its west to its east. Thank God for that."[18]

"Terrorism is as much about the threat of violence as the violent act itself," says terrorism expert, Bruce Hoffman.[19] A goal of terrorism is to cause fear.

CHAPTER 2

What Is Terrorism?

TERRORISM IS AN ACT OR THREAT OF VIOLENCE FOR A political, social, or religious purpose. It is designed to cause fear in a larger audience. In 2003, 4,271 people died from terrorist attacks worldwide.[1] This is far fewer than those killed in car accidents. Car accidents kill around forty-two thousand people yearly in the United States alone.[2] Still, people feel more threatened by terrorism. Some definitions include the idea that the victims are civilians.

Burglary, kidnapping, hostage-taking, hijacking, and murder can all sometimes be considered terrorism. But terrorism differs from ordinary criminal acts in terms of motive. Ordinary criminals act for selfish reasons, such as getting money or personal revenge. Terrorists have a message. They use shocking measures to get attention for their cause.

Hostage-takers and hijackers often have demands for the release of their hostages. Terrorism also takes the form of warlike acts. In 2003, 119 of the 208 international terrorist attacks were bombings.[3] Some terrorists use military terms and may think of themselves as freedom fighters. However, there are rules for war, which terrorists frequently break. Some of these rules are part of what are known as the Geneva and Hague conventions. They protect diplomats, neutral states, and embassies from attack and prohibit taking civilians as hostages. If these rules are broken, the people responsible can be tried for war crimes.

In addition, rules for war define the type of weapons that are reasonable. Chemical weapons, such as nerve gas, and biological weapons that spread disease are considered beyond the scope of warfare. These weapons target civilians or can spread to civilian areas. Most terrorist attacks have not used these weapons of mass destruction (WMDs), but some have.

In 1995, a Japanese religious cult called Aum Shinrikyo released a deadly nerve gas called sarin in the Tokyo subway system. Sarin affects the body's "off switch" for glands and muscles. Without the "off switch," the muscles are stimulated until they tire. Then, movement declines, vision fades, and even breathing stops.[4]

"After a few minutes I started to feel sick," said one

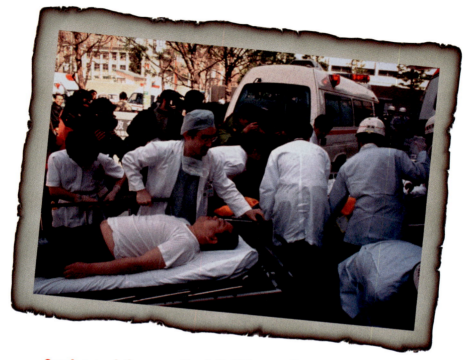

Survivors of the gas attack in Tokyo arrive at the St. Luke's International Hospital. Years after the attack, many survivors still suffered from the physical effects of the sarin gas.

survivor being treated in a Tokyo hospital after the attack. "My eyesight ha[d] gone dark, as though I [was] looking through a tunnel."[5]

"When I got to the hospital I couldn't move my hands enough to write my name, and I could barely speak," reported another survivor.[6] The sarin attack killed twelve people and injured thousands. But it could have been much worse. One of the biggest concerns in the fight against terrorism is that an attack using weapons of mass destruction could kill thousands.

Why Do Terrorists Act?

Terrorists have political, social, or religious goals behind their actions. Some terrorist groups are nationalist/separatist movements. They strive to hold land and leadership by creating independent countries. Terrorists that want to see Chechnya independent from Russia frequently attack the Russian capital of Moscow.

Chechen terror attacks have continued to escalate. In September 2004, terrorists stormed a school just outside the Chechen border. It was the first day of classes. Children and parents had gathered in an assembly hall to greet their teachers with flowers.

The terrorists burst in, heavily armed. Some wore explosive belts. They wired the gymnasium with bombs and threatened to destroy the school if any rescue attempt was made. The terrorists said "they would kill 50 hostages for each one of them killed, 20 for each wounded," reported an officer at the scene.[7]

When soldiers heard an explosion they rushed into the school. A fire fight started and chaos followed. In the end, more than 300 people died. Many were children. "Even alongside the most cruel attacks of the past, this

Fearful of a blast, a boy hostage holds his ears. The Chechen terrorist at the left has his left foot on a book which is rigged to a device that can set off a chain of explosives.

terrorist act occupies a special place because it was aimed at children," said Russian President Vladimir Putin.[8]

Other separatist movements, such as the IRA (Irish Republican Army), have been fighting for decades. The aims of these groups are political, but they have strong religious elements as well. In Ireland, terrorism grew out of conflict between Catholics and Protestants. The violence peaked in 1972 when 467 people were killed in one year. One attack known as Bloody Friday left 9 dead and 130 injured when 22 IRA bombs went off in 75 minutes.

17

In 1998, Britain and the IRA signed a peace agreement. Six months later, a small group of former IRA members known as the RIRA (Real Irish Republican Army) attacked the City of Omagh. A car bomb exploded in a busy shopping center. A phone call warning police misdirected people toward the blast instead of away from it. "They moved everyone toward the danger," said a local pub owner. "Then the explosion came right in the middle of the crowd."[9]

Religion and Terrorism

Islam, Judaism, and Christianity all have extreme offshoots or sects that have committed acts of terrorism. Some religious terrorists believe that they are acting on orders from God. Terrorism with religious motives includes the attack by Aum Shinrikyo in Japan and the Al Qaeda attacks on 9/11.

"We are fighting to wipe out the enemy."

—Former leader of Hezbollah, a terrorist group.

Religious terrorism is not new. The Zealots were an ancient Jewish sect that existed around 66 A.D. They were angry at the Roman occupation of what is now Israel. The Zealots slit the throats of Romans and Jewish supporters of Rome. They did this during daylight and in public areas to cause fear. Today, the word "zealot" means someone who is excessively religious.

The word "assassin," which today means a person hired to commit murder, comes from an ancient Muslim sect that existed from the eleventh to thirteenth centuries. Under the influence of a drug, the assassins were taken to a beautiful garden filled with pleasures. They were told that when they completed their mission, they would return to the garden. Today, a belief in a heavenly reward for suicide missions is still common.

Religious terrorists often see "nonbelievers" as less than human or evil. Their goal may be to eliminate certain races or religions.

Islamic Shi'a groups, such as Lebanon's Hezbollah and Palestine's HAMAS, want to spread an extreme view of Islamic law. "We are not fighting so that the enemy recognizes us and offers us something," said a former leader of Hezbollah. "We are fighting to wipe out the enemy."[10]

Religious terrorism is often carried out on a bigger scale than political terrorism. Terrorist experts used to think that "terrorists wanted a lot of people watching and listening, but not a lot of people dead."[11] This has changed. Now, terrorists want a lot of people dead as well.

CHAPTER

3

HAMAS and Israel

IN MARCH 2004, A SIXTEEN-YEAR-OLD PALESTINIAN boy wearing an oversized red jersey approached a checkpoint in Israel's West Bank. The checkpoint restricts who can enter the Israeli areas. The Israelis say that the checkpoints are for protection. But the Palestinians who are frequently denied access or subjected to long waits say that these restrictions limit their access to schools, jobs, and even necessary medical treatments.[1]

The boy looked suspicious to Lieutenant Tamir Milrad. "We saw that he had something under his shirt." The Israeli soldiers pointed their guns and took cover behind the concrete barricades. They ordered the boy to stop and take off the jersey. Beneath it was a vest containing an 18-pound (8-kilogram) bomb.

"He told us he didn't want to die. He didn't want to blow up," said Lieutenant Milrad.[2]

Terrorists often commit suicide attacks by filling a vest or a belt with explosives. This bomb belt was found in Fallujah, Iraq, by the United States Marines.

The potential attack came as Palestinians cried for revenge for the slaying of HAMAS leader Sheik Ahmed Yassin by the Israelis. Yassin, a spiritual leader, was killed in his wheelchair by missiles fired from Israeli helicopters. Israeli Prime Minister Ariel Sharon called Yassin "the mastermind of Palestinian terror and a mass murderer who is among Israel's greatest enemies." But for Abdel Aziz al-Rantissi who became the new HAMAS leader, "it's a war on Islam . . . they wanted to assassinate the Palestinian cause."[3] Abdel Aziz al-Rantissi was killed in a subsequent Israeli attack about a month later.

HAMAS, which means "zeal," sees the conflict between Israel and Palestine as a holy war. To many

Sheik Ahmed Yassin, the founder of the group HAMAS, was killed by Israelis in 2003.

Palestinians, HAMAS is fighting for their independence. The Palestinians lived in the area prior to the creation of Israel but do not have their own country. They do not have freedom and many live in poverty.

But to the Israelis, HAMAS is a terror group responsible for hundreds of attacks. In 2003, HAMAS carried out 150 attacks, including a suicide bombing on a Jerusalem bus that killed 17 people and wounded 84.[4]

"When I turned around I saw parts of the bus flying everywhere. I got out of the car and ran," said Jacob Bitnovsky, who was driving a car in front of the bus.[5] The attack came only a few months into a Palestinian cease-fire.

"There cannot be a peace process when there is a death process," said Prime Minister Ariel Sharon's adviser Dore Gold.[6]

Israel has repeatedly retaliated for terrorist attacks with missile strikes, armored bulldozer and tank invasions, and further restrictions.

In March 2004, Israel raided the Rafah refugee camp. The assault started with two missile attacks outside a mosque. As people rushed to help the men who were hit, two more missiles were fired. Six Palestinians were killed and the mosque was set ablaze.

The assault continued. Helicopter gunships riddled buildings with bullets. Israeli bulldozers tore up roads and soldiers searched houses in the nearby area of Tel Sultan. In all, Israeli fire killed nineteen Palestinians.[7]

Still, many Israelis and Palestinians want to end the cycle of violence. In 2003, United States President George W. Bush outlined a "road map" for peace. He stated that "[t]he Palestine state must be a reformed and peaceful and democratic state that abandons forever the use of terror. The government of Israel, as the terror-

ist threat is removed and security is improved, must take concrete steps to support the emergence of a viable and credible Palestinian state."[8]

A HAMAS militant holds a rocket-propelled grenade launcher. His headband reads "No God but God and Mohammed is the Prophet of Allah, al-Qassam brigade, Hamas militant wing."

CHAPTER

4

Al Qaeda Attacks

ON AUGUST 7, 1998, TWO MEN IN A TRUCK FILLED with several hundred pounds of explosives drove up to the gate of the American Embassy in Kenya. They were a part of an organization called Al Qaeda. One man jumped out throwing homemade stun grenades and yelling at the guards to open the gate. The guards stood their ground, but the bomb in the truck exploded at approximately 10:30 A.M.

Embassy spokesman Bill Barr heard a loud thump. "That was an explosion," he recalled someone saying. Then there was a larger explosion and everything went crazy. "We crawled out down the stairs in darkness. There was a lot of dust. We couldn't see," said Barr.[1]

Outside it was much worse. Buildings around the bomb site were a pile of twisted metal and broken concrete. At least fifty-three buildings were damaged. Windows

were shattered ten blocks away. Twelve Americans and 201 Kenyans died in the terrorist attack.

Less than ten minutes later, a bomb went off in front of the U.S. Embassy in Tanzania. This bomb killed eleven Tanzanians and took down most of the embassy. "This appears to have been a very well coordinated, very well planned attack— clearly not the work of amateurs," said then-National Security Council spokesperson P. J. Crowley.[2]

Days later, rescue teams were still digging people out from the wreckage. Investigators with trained dogs looked for clues. FBI spokesman Frank Scafidi explained that their top priority was to determine the type of explosive and the vehicle that brought it there. "[Those items] can be like a fingerprint of who did it."[3]

President Bill Clinton announced that he had obtained

information linking Osama bin Laden, the multimillionaire terrorist leader of Al Qaeda, to the embassy attacks. Clinton ordered a cruise missile attack on Al Qaeda training camps in Afghanistan and a possible terrorist laboratory in Sudan. But it was not enough.

Two years later, Osama bin Laden and Al Qaeda were connected to the bombing of the naval vessel the U.S.S. *Cole*. The *Cole* was refueling in Yemen. A small fishing boat with 500 to 700 pounds of explosives sidled up to the huge warship. The terrorists waved to those on deck.

Military investigators inspect the hole in the hull of the U.S.S. *Cole* in Aden, Yemen.

Then they blew a forty-by-sixty-foot hole in the *Cole*. The attack killed seventeen American sailors.

What Is Al Qaeda?

Al Qaeda ("the base") is a loosely-knit group of Islamic terrorists that grew out of the fight to remove the Soviet Union from Afghanistan. Some Islamic militants viewed the struggle as a holy war. They left their countries and went to Afghanistan to join the battle. After nearly ten years of fighting, the Soviet forces withdrew.

The Islamic militants returned home feeling triumphant. But at home, they were viewed with suspicion because of their extreme ideas. Cut off from their society, many became ready recruits for new campaigns and people such as Osama bin Laden.[4]

Osama bin Laden is Al Qaeda's spiritual leader and financier. He grew up rich and religious in Saudi Arabia. He fought in Afghanistan where his beliefs grew stronger and more radical. After the war, bin Laden focused his hate on a new enemy, the United States of America.

In 1996, he called for a *jihad* or holy war on Americans because of the U.S. support of Israel and the military presence in Saudi Arabia. Saudi Arabia is home to the two most holy places in Islam, Mecca and Medina. But most Muslims do not support violence. As President George W. Bush noted, ". . . the face of terror is not the

Osama bin Laden appeared on a video about a month after the September 11th attacks in 2001. He spoke out against America while holding a gun and wearing camouflage.

true face of Islam. Islam is a faith that brings comfort to a billion people around the world . . . It's a faith based upon love, not hate."[5]

Osama bin Laden does not share that view of Islam. In 1997, bin Laden called upon "every Muslim. . . to abide by Allah's order by killing Americans and stealing their money anywhere, any time, and whenever possible."[6]

In Afghanistan, bin Laden formed a relationship with the Taliban. The Taliban, with similar views of Islam, emerged from the subsequent Afghani civil wars as the party in power. The Taliban offered Osama bin Laden a safe haven. More than that, they offered Al Qaeda a place to train recruits in the methods of terror. U.S. intelligence estimates that ten to twenty thousand recruits went through instruction in bin Laden's training camps between 1996 and the attack on September 11, 2001.[7]

Al Qaeda After 9/11

After 9/11, President George W. Bush and the prime minister of Britain, Tony Blair, issued the Taliban an ultimatum: They could either "surrender the terrorists or surrender power."[8] The Taliban refused to give up the terrorists.

The United States and their British allies attacked Afghanistan with guided missiles fired from nearby warships.

Soldiers of the 82nd Airborne Division of the Army investigate a cave in Afghanistan. Many members of the Taliban and Al Qaeda hid in caves near the border of Afghanistan and Pakistan.

The initial targets were the Taliban's air defense, military command posts, and Al Qaeda training camps.

"Our objective is to defeat those who use terrorism and those who house or support them," said Secretary of Defense Donald Rumsfeld. "This is not about a single individual. It is about an entire terrorist network and multiple terrorist networks across the globe."[9]

Around the world, terrorist suspects were captured and Al Qaeda's abilities weakened. Taliban rule fell in Afghanistan, but bin Laden remained hidden. In March 2003, Khalid Shaik Mohammed, bin Laden's right-hand man, was captured. This led some to believe that "the tide had turned in terms of al Qaeda."[10]

But most terrorism experts were quick to caution against thinking that Al Qaeda was defeated. "Terrorist groups seldom quit, and al Qaeda did not retire on September 12," wrote terrorist expert Brian Jenkins.[11]

"Although al Qaeda has been damaged by the American-led campaign, it continues to benefit from its image as a powerful Islamic force that is capable of inflicting devastating blows on its foes," said Jenkins. "Al Qaeda, its associates, and its successors will fight on."[12]

Domestic Terrorism

DOMESTIC TERRORISM IS TERRORISM WHOSE ORIGINS are within the country of attack and have no foreign direction. In the United States, the most devastating occurrence of domestic terrorism was the bombing of the Alfred P. Murrah Federal Building in Oklahoma City.

Timothy McVeigh based his attack plan on a book called *The Turner Diaries*. McVeigh filled a Ryder truck

Timothy McVeigh was tried and executed for blowing up the Alfred P. Murrah Federal Building in Oklahoma City.

31

In the weeks after the attack in Oklahoma City, construction crews tried to clear rubble away from the blast site. Most of the Federal Building had been blown away.

with close to 4,300 pounds of fertilizer and fuel oil and left it near the Federal Building in Oklahoma City.

The explosion ripped off a side of the building. Floors collapsed on top of each other, crushing those in between. A day-care center was on the ground floor. More than 850 people were injured and 168 people died. Nineteen of them were children.

Carole Lawton was sitting at her desk on the seventh floor when "all of a sudden the windows blew in. It got real dark and the ceiling just started coming down." Then she heard "the roar of the whole building crumbling."[3]

Timothy McVeigh was a part of a growing militia movement in the United States. Many of these groups are racist. They view nonwhites and Jews as inferior. Other militia groups believe that the government is interfering with their freedom.

Acting Alone

Like Timothy McVeigh, individuals or pairings of two or three are increasingly engaging in terrorist-like violence. These individuals may not be involved with a larger political movement, but they are often inspired by it.[5]

The "Unabomber," Theodore Kaczynski, eluded arrest for seventeen years. During that time, he made over fifteen bombs that killed three people and wounded twenty-three others. He wrote a thirty-five-thousand-word manifesto to *The Washington Post* warning

Ted Kaczynski, the Unabomber, was once a professor at the University of California at Berkeley. He had graduated from Harvard and was considered a genius by some. However, he soon became a deadly terrorist.

John Allen Muhammad is escorted into court for his trial. His fellow sniper, Lee Boyd Malvo, is pictured in the inset.

about the evils of technology. He promised to stop his attacks if it was published. The letter led to his arrest. His brother recognized the writing and notified the FBI.

John Allen Muhammad, forty-one, and seventeen-year-old John Lee Malvo nearly paralyzed Washington, D.C., suburbs with fourteen sniper shootings before being caught. Schools were locked down as the two men randomly killed people in public areas like gas stations and parking lots. "People [were] just terrified to do things," said psychotherapist Jerilyn Ross. "Whether it's going to the grocery store, or sending their kids to school. I think that the whole city has really been terrorized."[6]

Defending Against Terrorism

AFTER 9/11, PRESIDENT GEORGE W. BUSH PLEDGED to direct "every resource at our command—every means of diplomacy, every tool of intelligence, every instrument of law enforcement, every financial influence, and every necessary weapon of war—to the disruption and to the defeat of the global terror network."[1]

Defending against terrorism happens on many fronts. Diplomacy creates communication between countries trying to defeat terrorism. Information is gathered and shared. Terrorists have fewer safe places to go because countries are working together to stop them.

Governments are also cutting terrorists off from their money supply. About 150 countries and jurisdictions have frozen terrorist-related financial assets.[2] Countries that pay

Several countries have pledged to fight terrorism alongside the United States. An Australian commando takes part in a counterterrorism exercise. He wears a gas mask, which would help protect him from a chemical or biological attack.

for terrorist attacks or provide places for terrorists to train or hide are being pressured to stop.

The 9/11 Commission was created to examine the events of 9/11. Their report offers many suggestions to make people safer. These recommendations include better screening at borders and airports, strengthening relationships with allies, and creating a National Counterterrorism Center.[3]

Everyday People Fighting Terrorism

Security expert Bruce Schneier says two of the most effective antiterrorism countermeasures aboard airlines after 9/11 were strengthening the cockpit doors and changing attitudes. Passengers learned that they needed to fight back.[4] That is what passengers did on Flight 63, December 23, 2001.

On a flight from Paris to Miami, Richard Reid tried to light his shoe with a match. Inside his shoes were explosives. A crew member smelled sulfur and saw a wire sticking out. She confronted Reid. Then, she yelled for help.

Eric Debry was sitting behind Reid. "I smelled some smoke, and then I heard a crying," Derby recalled. "I just jumped on his shoulders . . . two other guys came and took his legs."[5] A crew member threatened to spray him with a fire extinguisher. Other people poured drinks on Reid. About twenty passengers handed over belts to tie him down.

Thierry Dugeon was ten rows behind when he heard the flight attendant scream. He rushed up the aisle. By the time he got there, two other men had already jumped on the man. "Everyone knew what we needed to do. He was real powerful, but we were five or six."[6] A doctor injected Reid with a sedative, and military jets ushered the plane to an emergency landing in Boston.

Richard Reid is taken to the State Police barracks. He was caught trying to light an explosive device on his shoe on a flight from Paris, France to Miami, Florida.

The Department of Homeland Security developed an advisory system to communicate the risk of terrorist attacks on the United States.

What Can You Do?

Some of the things you can do to prepare for a terrorist attack are the same as for a natural disaster, such as preparing a supply kit or making a communication plan with your family.[7]

Long tones heard on the radio are often tests of the Emergency Broadcast System (EBS). The EBS helps people stay informed in the event of an emergency. Keeping a portable radio and extra batteries with supplies, including food and water, is a good idea.

Some terrorist threats, such as chemical attacks or biological weapons, can affect the air we breathe. If this occurs, make a barrier between yourself and the air. Placing a mask or scarf over your nose and mouth may help. Masks can be found in hardware stores and most grocery stores.

"Understanding and tolerance among people of different faiths can and must prevail."

—Excerpt from *The 9/11 Commission Report*

Being prepared in the event of a disaster is very important. But people are working to stop terrorism before it occurs. You can too. Respect and understanding are crucial to ending terrorism. As the *9/11 Commission Report* says, "Understanding and tolerance among people of different faiths can and must prevail."[8] When people see each other as equals or better yet friends, hatred will not take hold. By standing up against hate and violence now, we help eliminate it in the future.

World's Deadliest Terrorist Attacks

Rank	Date	Place	Description	Deaths*
1.	September 11, 2001	New York City, New York; Alexandria, Virginia; and western Pennsylvania	Hijacked planes were intentionally crashed into the World Trade Center (N.Y.), the Pentagon (Va.), and a field in Pennsylvania. The two largest World Trade Center towers collapsed.	3,212
2.	August 20, 1978	Abadan, Iran	A theater was set on fire.	477
3.	September 1–3, 2004	Beslan, Russia	Hostages were taken at a school. Bombs were exploded and people were shot.	359
4.	June 23, 1985	Over Ireland	An Air India flight was bombed.	329
5.	March 12, 1993	Mumbai, India	Fifteen bombs were exploded.	at least 260
6.	December 21, 1988	Over Lockerbie, Scotland	Pan Am Flight 103 was bombed.	270
7.	August 8, 1998	Nairobi, Kenya, and Dar es Salaam, Tanzania	Bombs in trucks exploded near two United States embassies.	224
8.	October 12, 2002	Kuta, Indonesia	Nightclub bombing	202
9.	March 11, 2004	Madrid, Spain	Bombing of several trains	191
10. (tie)	September 19, 1989	Over Chad	Bombing of French UTA flight	170
10. (tie)	October 26, 2002	Moscow, Russia	Hostage taking and attempted rescue in theater	170

*All figures include terrorists killed.

Chapter Notes

Chapter 1. Terrorism Strikes

1. David Handschuh, "A Lens on Life and Death," *At Ground Zero*, ed. Chris Bull and Sam Erman (New York: Thunder Mouth Press, 2002), p. 4.

2. L. A. Johnson and Barbara White Stack, "Local Eyewitnesses Describe Horror and Terror in New York," *Pittsburgh Post Gazette*, September 11, 2001, p. A6.

3. Jim Dwyer and Ford Fessenden, "Lost Voices of Firefighters, Some on the 78th Floor," *The New York Times*, August 4, 2002, p 1.1.

4. Shankar Vedantam, "Fear on the 86th Floor; James Gartenberg Called Friends, Family for Help—and Then Silence," *The Washington Post*, September 15, 2001, p. A01.

5. National Commission on Terrorist Attacks Upon the United States, *The 9/11 Commission Report*, p. 9, July 22, 2004, <http://www.9-11commission.gov/report/911Report.pdf> (October 20, 2004).

6. Ibid, p. 10.

7. Geraldine Baum and Matea Gold, "Terrorism Hits the U.S.; A day of Carnage and Chaos; Scene: Shock, incomprehension prevail as trade center, Pentagon burn," *The Los Angeles Times*, September 11, 2001, p. S1.

8. Helen O'Neill, "Everyone was Screaming, Crying, Running," *The San Diego Union–Tribune*, September 11, 2001, EXTRA, p. 83.

9. Baum and Gold, p. S1.

10. Vedantam, p. A01.

11. National Commission on Terrorist Attacks Upon the United States, p. 12.

12. Ibid., p. 13.

13. "LAST WORDS," *The Boston Globe*, September 16, 2001, p. D6.

14. National Commission on Terrorist Attacks Upon the United States, p. 14.

15. United States Department of State, "September 11, 2001: Basic Facts," August 15, 2002, <http://www.state.gov/coalition/cr/fs/12701.htm> (October 20, 2004).

16. Mary Jo Fox, personal interview, October 2003.

17. "Bin Laden Wanted Dead or Alive," *Milwaukee Sentinel Journal*, September 18, 2001, p. 01A.

18. Michael Kelly, "There's No Confusion Now," *Milwaukee Sentinel Journal*, October 10, 2001, p. 15A.

19. Bruce Hoffman, *Inside Terrorism* (New York: Columbia University Press, 1998), p. 38.

Chapter 2. What Is Terrorism?

1. United States Department of State, "The Year in Review (Revised)," *Patterns of Global Terrorism 2003*, June 22, 2004, <http://www.state.gov/s/ct/rls/pgtrpt/2003/33771.htm> (October 20, 2004).

2. National Center for Health Statistics, phone call with author.

3. United States Department of State.

4. "Facts about Sarin," *Centers for Diseases Control and Prevention*, March 7, 2003, <http://www.bt.cdc.gov/agent/sarin/basics/facts.asp> (October 20, 2004).

5. Charles Radin, "Poison Gas Assaults Tokyo six killed, 900 sent to hospitals after attack on subways; terrorism suspected," *Boston Globe*, March 20, 1995, p. 1.

6. Associated Press, "Nerve Gas Kills Six on Subway in Tokyo; 3,200 ill; terrorism is suspected; hospitals overwhelmed," *Buffalo News*, March 20, 1995, p. A1.

7. Peter Baker and Susan Glasser, "Hundreds Held Hostage at School in Russia; Many Children Seized In Town Near Chechnya," *The Washington Post*, September 2, 2004, p. A01.

8. Michael Eckel, "Chaos and Bloodshed; soldiers storm school, end siege," *Desert News*, September 4, 2004, p. A01.

9. T. R. Reid, "Marketplace Car Bomb Kills 28 in N. Ireland; Police say warning call sent victims to danger," *The Washington Post*, August 16, 1998, p. A01.

10. Bruce Hoffman, *Inside Terrorism* (New York: Columbia University Press, 1998), p. 96.

11. "Rethinking Terrorism in Light of the War on Terrorism," Testimony of Dr. Bruce Hoffman before the Subcommittee on Terrorism and Homeland Security, September 26, 2001.

Chapter 3. HAMAS and Israel

1. Martin Asser, "Guide to a West Bank Checkpoint," *BBC News*, n.d., <http://news.bbc.co.uk/1/shared/spl/hi/middle_east/03/w_bank_checkpoints/html/default.stm> (October 20, 2004).

2. Gavin Rabinowitz, "Detained Palestinian Teen in Bomb Vest Disarms as Cameras Roll," *St. Louis Post–Dispatch*, March 25, 2004, p. A14.

3. Donald Macintyre, "The cry of vengeance; Palestinians vow 'war on the sons of Zion' after Israel unleashes fury in Gaza with the assassination of the spiritual leader of Hamas," *The Independent*, London, March 23, 2004, p. 1.4.

4. United States Department of State, "Middle East Overview," *Patterns of Global Terrorism 2003*, April 29, 2004, <http://www.state.gov/s/ct/rls/pgtrpt/2003/31638.htm> (October 20, 2004).

5. Eric Silver, "'We thought ceasefire meant we could relax. How wrong we were'; Jerusalem Bus Bomb," *The Independent*, London, August 20, 2003, p.10.

6. Michael Matza and Soraya Sarhaddi Nelson, "Suicide bomber kills 20 in Jerusalem," *Milwaukee Journal Sentinel*, August 20, 2003, p. 1A.

7. Damien Henderson and Kevin Frayer, "Tears Flow at End of Rafah Rainbow; Offensive in refugee camp leaves 19 dead," *The Herald*, Glasgow, May 19, 2004, p. 7.

8. Office of the Press Secretary, "President Discusses Road Map for Peace in the Middle East," *The White House*, March 14, 2003, <http://www.whitehouse.gov/news/releases/2003/03/20030314-4.html> (October 20, 2004).

Chapter 4. Al Qaeda Attacks

1. Karin Davies, "Witnesses Describe Bombings," *Sunday Gazette—Mail*, Charleston, August 9, 1998, p. 1A.

2. Staff and Wire Report, "Embassy Bombings 81 Dead, 1,715 Hurt; Simultaneous Blasts Draw Worldwide Condemnation" *Virginian–Pilot: Norfolk*, August 8, 1998, p. A1.

3. Edith Lederer, "Bomb Sites Combed for Clues; Survivors Search," *Times–Picayune*, New Orleans, August 9, 1998, p. A1.

4. Brian Jenkins, *Countering Al Qaeda* (Santa Monica: RAND, 2002), p. 3.

5. National Commission on Terrorist Attacks Upon the United States, *The 9/11 Commission Report*, p. 54, July 22, 2004, <http://www.9-11commission.gov/report/911Report.pdf> (October 20, 2004).

6. Peter Bergen, *Holy War Inc., Inside the World of Osama bin Laden* (New York: The Free Press, 2001), p. 98.

7. National Commission on Terrorist Attacks Upon the United States, p. 67.

8. Mike Allen, "Bush, Blair warn Taliban of Retaliation," *The Washington Post*, October 3, 2001, p. A01.

9. Michael Hedges, "America Responds/Counterattack/ Tons of bombs pound Afghanistan as fight escalates," *Houston Chronicle*, October 8, 2001, p. 1.

10. Dana Priest and Susan Schmidt, "Al Qaeda's Top Primed to Collapse, U.S. Says; Mohammed's Arrest, Data Breed Optimism," *The Washington Post*, March 16, 2003, p. A01.

11. Jenkins, p. 8.

12. Ibid., pp. 9, 15.

Chapter 5. Domestic Terrorism

1. Walter Laqueur, *The New Terrorism* (Oxford: Oxford University Press, 1999), p. 115.

2. Lou Michel and Dan Herbeck, *American Terrorist: Timothy McVeigh and the Oklahoma City Bombing* (New York: ReganBooks, 2001), p. 39.

3. Rochelle Hines, "Terrorists Strike U. S. Heartland," *Toronto Star*, April 20, 1995, p. A1.

4. Bruce Hoffman, *Al Qaeda, Trends in Terrorism, and Future Potentialities: An Assessment* (Santa Monica: RAND, 2003), p. 115.

5. Ibid., p. 17.

6. Shira Kantor, "As Fear Mounts, Routines Change; Virginia shooting marks 7th fatality in weeklong spree," *Chicago Tribune*, October 11, 2002, p. 1.

Chapter 6. Defending Against Terrorism

1. President George W. Bush, Address to Joint Session of Congress September 20, 2001, from United States Department of State, "Preface and Introduction," *Patterns of Global Terrorism 2001*, May 21, 2002, <http://www.state.gov/s/ct/rls/pgtrpt/2001/html/10220.htm> (October 20, 2004).

2. United States Department of State, "Introduction," *Patterns of Global Terrorism 2003*, April 24, 2004, <http://www.state.gov/s/ct/rls/pgtrpt/2003/31880.htm> (October 20, 2004).

3. National Commission on Terrorist Attacks Upon the United States, *The 9/11 Commission Report*, pp. 361–428, July 22, 2004, <http://www.9-11commission.gov/report/911Report.pdf> (October 20, 2004).

4. Bruce Schneier, *Beyond Fear* (New York: Copernicus Books, 2003), p. 248.

5. Dana Canedy, "A 'Strange' Traveler Acted, And the Passengers Reacted," *New York Times*, December 24, 2001, p. A1.

6. Pam Belluck, "Crew Grabs Man; Explosive Feared," *The New York Times*, December 23, 2001, p. 1A1.

7. "Preparing makes sense. Get Ready Now," *U.S. Department of Homeland Security*, n.d., <http://www.ready.gov/index.html> (October 20, 2004). [This Web site has information on how to create a supply kit and a communications plan.]

8. National Commission on Terrorist Attacks Upon the United States, p. 363.

Glossary

barricade—A protective barrier.

campaign—Planned organized series of actions, usually involving fighting.

civilian—An ordinary citizen; not a member of the armed forces.

diplomacy—Conducting relations between nations.

evacuate—To leave or make empty.

extremist—A person carried away beyond reason by feelings or beliefs.

ideological—A belief in an ideal or perfection often having to do with a perfect society.

manifesto—A written declaration of principles, policies, and objectives.

militant—Someone extremely active in the defense or support of a cause.

mosque—A building where Muslims worship.

poverty—The state of being poor.

psychological—Affecting the mind.

racist—Someone who treats people unfairly because of their race or religion.

retaliate—To strike back often as revenge for a previous harm.

supremacist—Someone who has a belief in a supreme group of people.

terrorism—A violent act with a political, social, or religious motive designed to cause fear.

ultimatum—A final offer or demand, the rejection of which usually leads to a break in relations or use of force.

Further Reading

Books

Fridell, Ron. *Terrorism: Political Violence at Home and Abroad.* Berkeley Heights, N.J.: Enslow Publishers, Inc., 2001.

Gow, Mary. *Attack on America: The Day the Twin Towers Collapsed.* Berkeley Heights, N.J.: Enslow Publishers, Inc., 2002.

Katz, Samuel M. *U.S. Counterstrike: American Counterterrorism.* Minneapolis, Minn.: Lerner Publications, 2005.

Roleff, Tamara, ed. *America Under Attack: Primary Sources.* San Diego, Calif.: Lucent Books, 2002.

Internet Addresses

National Commission on Terrorist Attacks Upon the United States
<http://www.9-11commission.gov/>
Download a copy of the 9/11 report.

Ready.gov—U.S. Department of Homeland Security
<http://www.ready.gov>
This Web site has information on what to do if there is a terrorist attack. It tells you what to include in a supply kit and how to make a family communication plan.

Terrorism Resource Center
<http://www.terrorism.com>
This site offers the latest news and research on terrorism.

Index